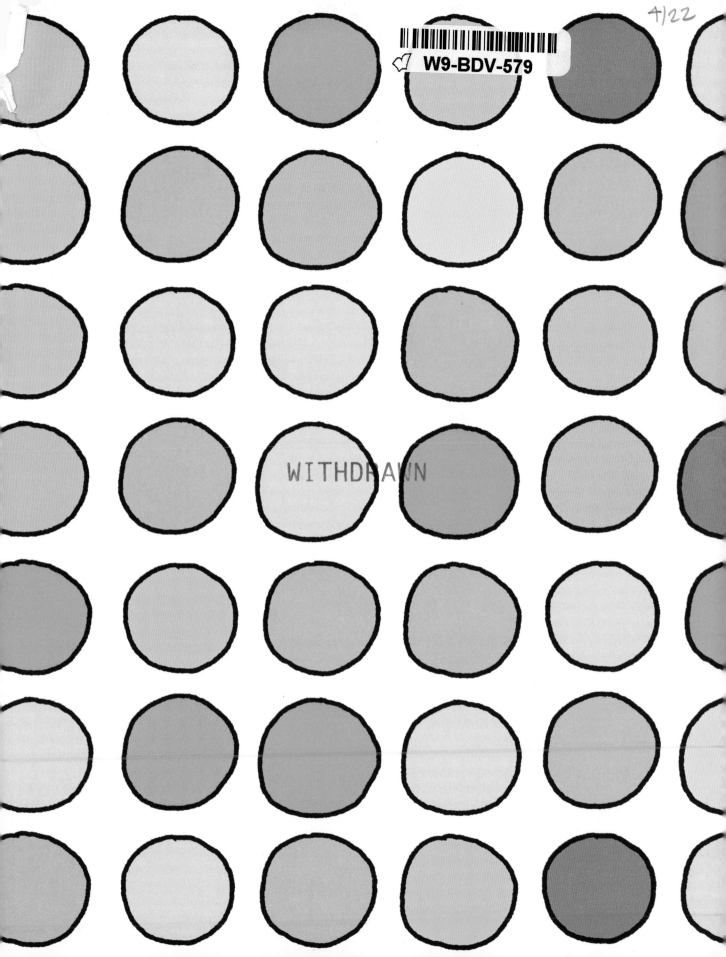

W9-BDV-579

WITHDRAWN

4/22

For Anne Schwartz
And in memory of RBG

Check out these organizations for additional information:

A Mighty Girl: amightygirl.com
Family Equality: familyequality.org
Gender Spectrum: genderspectrum.org
GLAAD: glaad.org
Let Toys Be Toys: lettoysbetoys.org.uk
PFLAG: pflag.org
Trans Youth Equality Foundation: transyouthequality.org
Welcoming Schools: welcomingschools.org

Copyright © 2022 by Elise Gravel

All rights reserved. Published in the United States by Anne Schwartz Books, an imprint of Random House Children's Books,
a division of Penguin Random House LLC, New York.
Anne Schwartz Books and the colophon are trademarks of Penguin Random House LLC.

Visit us on the Web! rhcbooks.com
Educators and librarians, for a variety of teaching tools, visit us at RHTeachersLibrarians.com

Library of Congress Cataloging-in-Publication Data is available upon request.
ISBN 978-0-593-17863-8 (trade) — ISBN 978-0-593-17864-5 (lib. bdg.) — ISBN 978-0-593-17865-2 (ebook)

The text of this book is set in 24-point Argone LC.
The illustrations were rendered in pen and ink and Adobe Photoshop.
Book design by Martha Rago

MANUFACTURED IN CHINA
10 9 8 7 6 5 4 3 2 1
First Edition

Random House Children's Books supports the First Amendment and celebrates the right to read.

Penguin Random House LLC supports copyright. Copyright fuels creativity, encourages diverse voices, promotes free speech,
and creates a vibrant culture. Thank you for buying an authorized edition of this book and for complying with copyright laws by
not reproducing, scanning, or distributing any part in any form without permission. You are supporting writers and allowing
Penguin Random House to publish books for every reader.

PINK, BLUE, AND YOU!

Questions for Kids
About Gender Stereotypes

Written and Illustrated by
ELISE GRAVEL
with Mykaell Blais

a·s·b
anne schwartz books

Look at these pictures. Are some for girls? Are some for boys? Are some for everyone?

Do we need to follow them?
What happens if we don't want to?

Have you heard people say any of these things?

Are these statements always TRUE?

Do you think everyone should be allowed to cry, play with dolls, and play sports if they feel like it?

The idea that we should follow different sets of rules can make us feel bad.

Should we feel bad about doing the things we like?

And what does it even mean
to be a

GIRL

or a

BOY?

Do we have to be one or the other?

Or can we be

BOTH at the same time,

or NEITHER?

We are born with small differences in our bodies.
This is our

SEX.

Grown-ups call us GIRL or BOY.

Scientists call us FEMALE or MALE.

A few of us are born in bodies that
aren't all female or male.
Scientists call us INTERSEX.

But who we are is way more complicated than these names.

When I was born, I was called a girl but I feel like a boy.

I don't really feel like a boy or a girl. I just want to be ME.

I feel like I'm both a boy and a girl at the same time.

The word that I like the most is **THEY.**

Little words like
HE, SHE, and THEY are called

PRONOUNS.

There are other pronouns, too. What pronoun
do you want people to use when they talk about you?

No matter who we are, what we like,
how we feel, how we dress, and
what our body looks like,
we ALL deserve to be
loved, protected, and respected.

Unfortunately, not everybody agrees.
Some people don't believe
that all humans should have
the same rights.

Throughout history, there have been laws and rules telling people how to behave. Women have been told that they shouldn't:

Men have been told that they shouldn't:

Do you think these laws and rules are fair?

Some governments even made laws telling people who they're allowed to fall in love with.

Do you think all people should be allowed to

LOVE WHOEVER THEY WANT?

♥

Some laws have prevented men who love men and women who love women from marrying or raising children. But in reality, there are many, many different ways to be a loving

FAMILY.

What is your family like?

Meanwhile, men are not encouraged to work in caregiving jobs. Most teachers, social workers, and nurses are women.

People with other gender identities are also not treated equally.

But there will always be brave people who follow their dreams despite what others think about them:

EDWARD T. LYON was the first male nurse in the US Army.

RICHARD JOHN BAKER & JAMES MICHAEL MCCONNELL were the first male couple to marry in the United States.

When she was little, **SARAH MCBRIDE** was called a boy. She was elected to the state senate of Delaware in 2020.

VALENTINA TERESHKOVA was the first woman in space.

WE'WHA was a Zuni Mexican whose sex was male but lived as a two-spirit, which is a third gender in some cultures.

MALALA YOUSAFZAI fought for the right for girls to go to school in her country.

Do you know anyone who followed their dreams?

The good news is that the world is changing.
It is easier to be who we really are, and we can
find friends and allies who support us.

Can you imagine how free we would feel
if things changed even more in the future?

Won't it be nice to live in a world where we can all just be

OURSELVES?

FUN FACTS

ABOUT GENDER AND CLOTHING

One hundred and fifty years ago, all little kids wore white frilly dresses and long hair. Here's a picture of Franklin Delano Roosevelt, a president of the United States, when he was four.

A hundred years ago, fashion magazines told parents that pink is for boys and blue is for girls.

Indian
mundu

Celtic
kilt

Sri Lankan
sarong

In many countries,
it's normal for men
to wear skirts.

In the popular TV show
Star Trek, male and female
crew members wore a dress
called a skant. It's a combo
of "skirt" and "pants."

In Persia, men wore high heels because
they made it easier to ride horses,
stand tall, and shoot arrows.

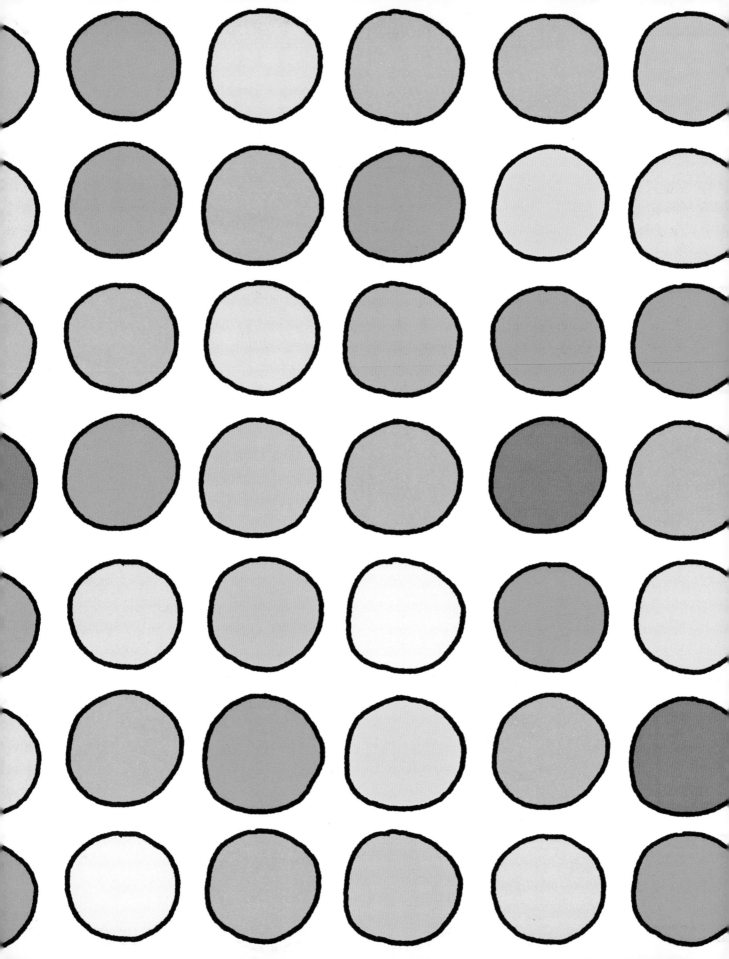